THE PERFUMED
GARDEN

WARNING: With the prevalence of AIDS and other sexually transmitted diseases, if you do not practice safe sex you are risking your life and your partner's life.

THE PERFUMED GARDEN

HarperSanFrancisco

A Division of HarperCollins*Publishers*

INTRODUCTION

'Let the world rain fire and brimstone on me now!' With these
words Lady Isabel Burton prepared herself for the fury that she
knew would follow the most notorious literary bonfire of all
time, a terrible act of destruction, in which she had burned Sir
Richard Burton's diaries, notebooks and letters, and his
thousand-page revision of 'The Perfumed Garden' completed the
day before he died on October 20th 1890.

Richard Burton – explorer, linguist and Orientalist – had
interrupted publication of his major work, the multi-volume
translation of The Arabian Nights, in order to produce the earlier
1886 version of The Perfumed Garden from which this selection
has been made. Much as The Arabian Nights borrowed tales
from India, we have used Indian miniatures to illustrate extracts
from the 1886 text because of course it is forbidden to depict the
human figure in Islamic art.

The Perfumed Garden (Men's Hearts to Gladden) was
certainly close to Richard Burton's heart: its unique literary blend
of sex, Arab folklore and sardonic humour was perfectly suited to
his temperament and interests. We shall never know what
Burton made of the revised manuscript, in which he worked
from the original Arabic and not the French version published by
'Baron R', ostensibly in Algiers, in 1850. What is clear even in
the earlier version is the extraordinary identification between the
author, Sheikh Nefzawi, and the translator, Richard Burton.

Perhaps it was this very identification – amounting almost to interchangeability – which so alarmed Lady Burton. Her husband's revision would have been fuller and more explicit than the version we have, and he had certainly re-instated the chapter on homosexuality from the original. Who knows what ghosts flitted about Isabel as she consigned the letters, notebooks and manuscript to the flames?

Sheikh Nefzawi tells us himself that he wrote The Perfumed Garden as a commission for the Grand Vizier of Tunis some time after the Spanish conquest of Algiers in 1510. His patron directed him to analyze 'the source of our greatest pleasure . . . in order that this knowledge should be widely known.' The fact that Sheikh Nefzawi was writing to please two audiences – an urbane politician for whom sex would have had few secrets and the uninitiated seeking sexual instruction – may explain the book's humour. That sex can be (and often is) funny is an important idea and an enabling one. Whether it comes from Sheikh Nefzawi or his alter ego Richard Burton, it is above all the humour of The Perfumed Garden which ensures its place among the world's classics.

DEDICATION

Praise be to God who has placed the source of man's greatest pleasure in woman's natural parts, and woman's greatest pleasure in the natural parts of man!

Who has decreed that the well-being, satisfaction and comfort of a woman's parts shall depend on the welcome they accord to the virile member, and that a man shall know neither rest nor peace till his duty has been nobly done!

THE BLESSING OF SEX

God has granted us the kiss on the mouth, the cheeks and the neck, as also the sucking of luscious lips, to provoke an erection at a favourable time. It is He, who, in His wisdom, has embellished with breasts a woman's chest, her neck with a double chin, and her cheeks with jewels and brilliants. He has also given her eyes which inspire love, and lashes sharp as polished blades. With admirable flanks and a delightful navel

He has heightened the beauty of her gently domed belly. He has endowed her with buttocks nobly planned, and has supported the whole on majestic thighs. Between these latter He has placed the field of strife which, when it abounds in flesh, resembles by its amplitude a lion's head. Its name among mankind is 'vulva'. Oh, how innumerable are the men who have died for this! how many, alas, of the bravest!

God has given this object a mouth, a tongue, two lips and a shape like unto the footprint of a gazelle on the sands of the desert.

CONCERNING PRAISEWORTHY MEN

Learn, Oh Vizier (may the blessing of God rest on you), that men and women are of divers kinds; some there are who are worthy of praise, while others deserve only censure.

When a worthy man is in the company of women his member grows, becomes strong, vigorous and hard; he is slow to ejaculate and, after the spasm caused by the emission of semen, he is prompt at re-erection.

A man so endowed will be dearly cherished.

For a man to be successful with women he must pay them marked attention. His dress should be neat, his figure graceful, and his looks should mark him out from his fellows. He must be truthful and sincere, generous and brave. He should not be vain, he should make himself agreeable in company. He must be the slave of his word; if he makes a promise he must keep it; he must always speak the truth and never fail to perform whatever he undertakes. He who boasts of his relations with women is contemptible.

CONCERNING THE GENERATIVE ACT

*Woman is like a fruit which will only yield its fragrance
when rubbed by the hands. Take, for example, the
basil: unless it be warmed by the fingers it emits no
perfume. And do you not know that unless amber be
warmed and manipulated it retains its aroma within?
The same with woman: if you do not animate her with
your frolics and kisses, with nibbling of her thighs and
close embraces, you will not obtain what you desire;
you will experience no pleasure when she shares your
couch and be sure that she will feel no affection for you.*

The things which develop love for the moment of coition are the playful frolics practised in advance, and the vigorous embrace at the moment of ejaculation. Believe me, kisses, nibblings, sucking of lips, close-clasping of breasts, and the drinking of passion-loaded spittle, are the things which ensure a durable affection. Acting thus, the two ejaculations occur simultaneously, and enjoyment is complete for both.

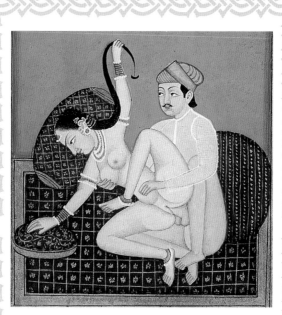

When, therefore, you see a woman's lips tremble and redden, and her eyes become languishing and her sighs profound, know that she desires coition; then is the time to get between her thighs and penetrate her. If you have followed my advice you will both enjoy a delightful copulation which will leave a delicious memory.

Someone has said: 'If you desire to copulate, place the woman on the ground, embrace her closely and put your lips on hers; then clasp her, suck her, bite her; kiss her neck, her breasts, her belly and her flanks; strain her to you until she lies limp with desire. When you see her in this state, introduce your member. If you act thus your enjoyment will be simultaneous, and this is the secret of pleasure. But if you neglect this plan the woman will not satisfy your desires, and she herself will gain no enjoyment.'

CONCERNING POSTURES

According to your taste you may choose the posture
which pleases you most, provided always that
intercourse takes place through the appointed organ:
the vulva.

First posture Lay the woman on her back and raise
her thighs; then, getting between her legs introduce
your member. Gripping the ground with your toes, you
will be able to move in a suitable manner. This posture
is a good one for those who have long members.

Second posture *If your member is short, lay the woman on her back and raise her legs in the air so that her toes touch her ears. Her buttocks being thus raised, the vulva is thrown forward. Now introduce your member.*

Third posture Lay the woman on the ground and get between her thighs; then putting one of her legs on your shoulder and the other under your arm, penetrate her.

Fourth posture Stretch the woman on the ground and put her legs on your shoulders; in that position your member will be exactly opposite her vulva which will be lifted off the ground. That is the moment for introducing your member.

Fifth posture Let the woman lie on her side on the ground; then lying down yourself and getting between her thighs, introduce your member. This posture is apt to give rise to rheumatic or sciatic pains.

Sixth posture Let the woman rest on her knees and elbows in the position for prayer. In this posture the vulva stands out behind. Approach her thus.

Seventh posture Lay the woman on her side, and then you yourself sitting on your heels will place her top leg on your nearest shoulder and her other leg against your thighs. She will keep on her side and you will be between her legs. Introduce your member and move her backwards and forwards with your hands.

Eighth posture Lay the woman on her back and kneel astride her.

Ninth posture Place the woman so that she rests,
either face forward or the reverse, against a slightly
raised platform, her feet remaining on the ground and
her body projecting in front. She will thus present her
vulva to your member which you will introduce.

Tenth posture Place the woman on a rather low divan
and let her grasp the woodwork with her hands; then,
placing her legs on your hips and telling her to grip
your body with them, you will introduce your member,
at the same time grasping the divan. When you begin
to work, let your movements keep time.

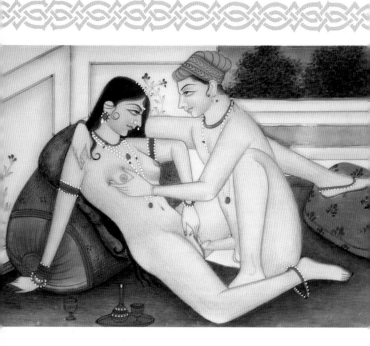

Eleventh posture *Lay the woman on her back and let
her buttocks be raised by a cushion placed under them.
Let her put the soles of her feet together: now get
between her thighs.*

There are other postures besides the preceding in use in India. It is well that you should know that the Hindus have greatly multiplied the ways of possessing a woman and have carried their investigations in this matter much farther than the Arabs. Among other postures and variations are the following:

The Archimedean screw *While the man is lying on his back the woman sits on his member, keeping her face towards his. She then places her hands on the bed, at the same time keeping her belly off his; she now moves up and down and, if the man is light in weight, he may move as well. If the woman wishes to kiss the man she need only lay her arms on the bed.*

The mutual view of the buttocks *The man lies on his back, and the woman, turning her back to him, sits on his member. He now clasps her body with his legs and she leans over until her hands touch the floor. Thus supported she has a view of his buttocks, and he of hers, and she is able to move conveniently.*

The sheep's posture The woman kneels down and puts her forearms on the ground; the man kneels down behind her and slips his penis in her vulva which she makes stand out as much as possible. His hands should be placed on her shoulders.

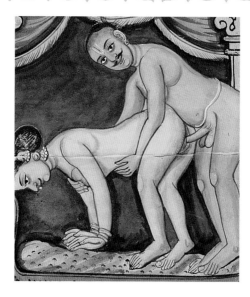

The camel's hump *The woman, who is standing,*
bends forward till her fingers touch the floor; the man
gets behind and copulates, at the same time grasping
her thighs. If the man withdraws while the woman is
still bending down, the vagina emits a sound like the
bleating of a calf, and for that reason many women
object to the posture.

CONCLUDING POSTURES

It is related that a man had a mistress of incomparable beauty, grace, and perfection. He was in the habit of copulating with her in the ordinary way to the exclusion of any other. The woman experienced none of the pleasure which should accompany the act, and was always ill-tempered afterwards. The man told his trouble to an old woman, who said: 'Try different methods of copulating with your mistress and see which gives her most pleasure. When you have found it, never use another, and she will love you without bounds.'

On Kissing

It is claimed by some that kissing is an integral part of copulation.

The most delightful kiss is that which is planted on moist ardent lips, and accompanied with suction of the lips and tongue, so that the emission of a sweet intoxicating saliva is produced. It is for the man to procure this emission from the woman by gently nibbling her lips and tongue till she secretes a particular saliva, sweet, exquisite, more agreeable than honey mixed with pure water, and which does not mix with her ordinary saliva. This gives the man a shivering sensation throughout his whole body, and is more intoxicating than strong wine.

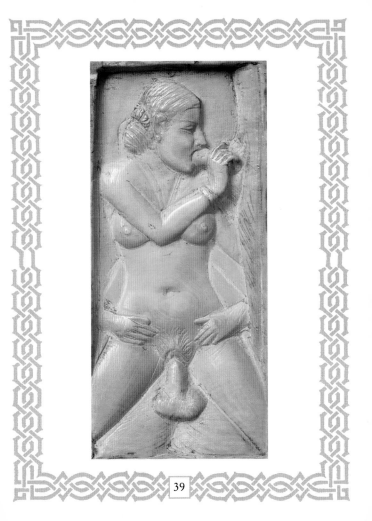

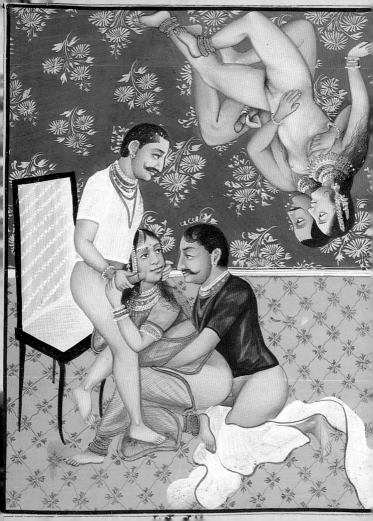

CONCERNING THE DIVERS NAMES OF THE VIRILE MEMBER

Know, oh Vizier (God grant you mercy!), that the virile member has many names, among which are the following:

*The virile member * Generative organ * **Smith's bellows** * **Pigeon** * **Jingler** * **Untameable** * **Liberator** * Creeper * Exciter * Deceiver * **Sleeper** * Pathmaker * **Tailor** * Quencher * Twister * **Knocker** * Swimmer * Enterer * Withdrawer * One-eyed * Bald-head * One with an eye * Stumbler * Funny-head * One with a neck * Hairy one * **Shameless one** * **Bashful one** * **Weeper** * Mover * **Annexer** * **Spitter** * **Splasher** * Breaker * **Seeker** * Rubber * Flabby one * Searcher * and Discoverer.*

The smith's bellows It has received this name because
of its alternative inflation and deflation.
The pigeon It is so called because, after having been
swollen and at the moment when it is returning to its
state of repose, it resembles a pigeon settling on its eggs.

The jingler It is so called on account of the noise it makes each time it enters or leaves the vulva.

The untameable It has received this name because, when it is swollen and erect, it starts to move its head, looking for the entrance to the vagina, which, when found, it brusquely and insolently enters.

The liberator *So named because when entering the vulva of a divorced woman, it frees her from the prohibition of remarrying her former husband.*

The sleeper *This name is due to its deceptive appearance. When it enters in erection it lengthens and stiffens to such a pitch that you would never think it would soften again, but, when it leaves the vulva after slaking it falls asleep.*

The tailor It gets this name from the fact that it does not enter the vulva until after it has manoeuvred at the entrance, like a needle in the hand of a tailor.

The knocker It is thus named because, when it arrives at the door of the vulva, it gives a light knock; if the vulva replies and opens the door, it enters; but, if it gets no reply, it knocks again until successful. By knocking at the door we refer to the rubbing of the penis on the vulva until it becomes moist. The production of this moisture is what is called opening the door.

The shameless one It has received this name because, from the minute it gets stiff and long, it cares for nobody. It unblushingly lifts its master's raiment, caring nought for the shame he feels. It acts in the same shameless way with a woman. It will lift her clothes and expose her thighs. Its master may feel shame at this conduct, but, as for itself, its stiffness and ardour go on increasing.

The bashful one This member, met with in some
individuals, feels shame and becomes bashful when in
the presence of an unknown vulva, and it is only after
a time that it raises its head. Sometimes its trouble is so
great that it remains quite impotent, especially if a
stranger is near.

The weeper So called because of the many tears it
sheds. As soon as it stands, it begins to weep; if it sees a
pretty face it weeps; if it touches a woman, it weeps. It
even at times weeps tears of remembrance.

The annexer This gets its name because when it enters the vulva, it starts to move, but, at the same time, clings closely hair to hair and even tries to force the testicles in.

The spitter It has received this name because, at the approach of the vulva or at its aspect, or even simply at its memory, or when its master touches a woman, plays with her or kisses her, its saliva begins to flow; this saliva is particularly abundant after a long abstinence and will sometimes soak the clothing.

This member is very common and few are the men not so endowed.

The splasher So called because it makes a splashing noise when it enters the vulva.

The seeker This name was given because, when it is in the vulva, it starts to move about as if it were looking for something. It is looking for the womb, and it has no peace till it finds it.

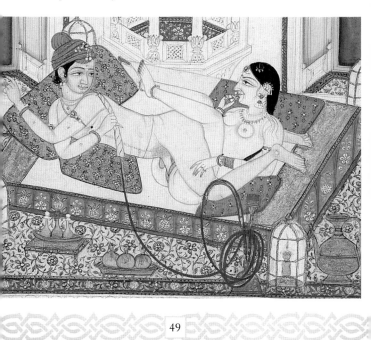

CONCERNING THE FEMALE ORGAN

The following are the usual names:
*The passage * Vulva * Libidinous * **Primitive** **
Starling * **Crested One** * **Snub-nosed** * **Hedgehog** **
Taciturn * **Squeezer** * Importunate * Sprinkler **
*Desirer * Beauty * **Sweller** * **High-brow** * Spreader **
*Giant * Glutton * Bottomless pit * Two-lipped one **
Camel's hump * **Sieve** * Mover * **Annexer** **
Accommodator * Helper * Arch * Extender * Duellist
** Ever-ready * Fleer * Resigned * Wet one **
*Barricaded one * Abyss * **Biter** * **Sucker** * **Wasp***
*Warmer * Delicious one.*

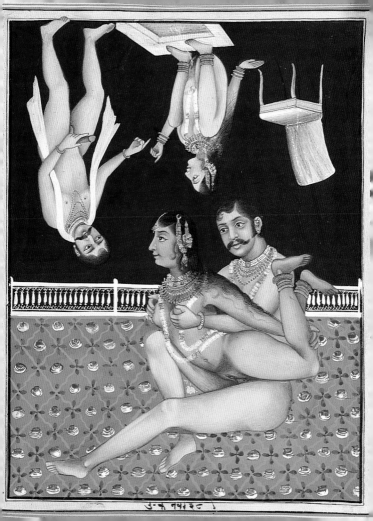

The primitive *This name is applicable to any vulva.*
The starling *Applied to a brunette's vulva.*
The crested one *This is provided with a comb like a cock's which stands up at the moment of pleasure.*
The snub-nosed *This has thin lips and a tiny tongue.*
The hedgehog *This is where the hair is exceptionally thick and ticklish.*

The taciturn *This is the one which is sparing in words.*
Should a member penetrate a hundred times a day it
would say nothing but would be content to look on.
The squeezer *So called because of its squeezing action*
on the member. Immediately after penetration it starts
to squeeze the member and draws it in with such gusto
that were it possible, it would absorb the testicles too.

The sweller So called because, when a member arrives at the entrance, it is caused to swell and stand up at once. It procures enormous satisfaction for its owner, and, at the moment of enjoyment, it winks.

The high-brow This is surmounted by a pubis which resembles a stately forehead.

The camel's hump This is crowned by a mons veneris which stands out like a camel's hump and which stretches between the thighs like a calf's head. God grant that we may enjoy such a vulva! Amen!

The sieve When this vulva receives a member it starts to move up and down, right and left, backwards and forwards, until complete satisfaction .

The annexer That vagina is so called, which when it has received a member, clings round it as closely as possible, so that, if it could, it would draw in the testicles.

The accommodator *This name is applied to the vagina of the woman who has felt for some time an ardent desire for coition. In its satisfaction at seeing a member, it aids it in its reciprocating movement; it eagerly offers the womb, and it could offer nothing more welcome.*

When the member wishes to visit any particular part it lends itself graciously to the task, so that no nook is left unvisited.

When enjoyment arrives and the member wishes to ejaculate, it clasps its head and presents the womb. It then vigorously sucks the member, using all its powers to extract the sperm destined to flow into the expectant womb. And certainly, pleasure is incomplete for the woman possessing such a vagina if the flood of semen is not poured into the womb.

The biter The one which, when the member has penetrated, burns with such passion that it opens and shuts on the member. Especially at the moment of ejaculation the man feels his member seized by the sucker which draws like a magnet and exhausts it of its sperm. If God in his power has decreed that the woman shall conceive, the sperm is concentrated in the woman, but if not it is expelled.

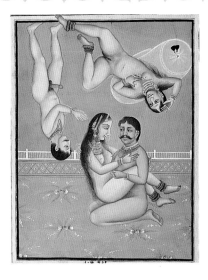

The sucker *This is the vagina which, dominated by amorous ardour resulting from continence or from frequent and voluptuous caresses, grasps the member and sucks it with a strength capable of draining its sperm, acting thus as a child who sucks its mother.*
The wasp *This vulva is known by the strength and hardness of the pubic hair. When the member approaches it gets stung as by a wasp.*

CONCERNING THE THINGS WHICH MAKE THE GENERATIVE ACT ENJOYABLE

Know, oh Vizier (God grant you His mercy!), that the things which tend to develop a passion for coition are six in number: an ardent love, an abundance of sperm, the propinquity of the person loved, beauty of face, a suitable diet, and contact.

The extreme pleasure which has its source in an impetuous and abundant ejaculation depends on one circumstance; it is imperative that the vagina be capable of suction. It then clings to the member and sucks out the semen by a irresistible attraction which is only comparable to that of a magnet.

Once the member is grasped by the sucker, the man can no longer prevent the emission of semen, and the member is tightly held until it is completely drained. However, if the man ejaculates before arousing the sucker, both parties derive but little pleasure from the act of coition.

In writing this book
I have sinned indeed!
Your pardon, oh Lord, I surely shall need;
But, if on the last day you absolve me, why then,
All my readers will join me
in a loud AMEN!